JUMPING SPIDERS

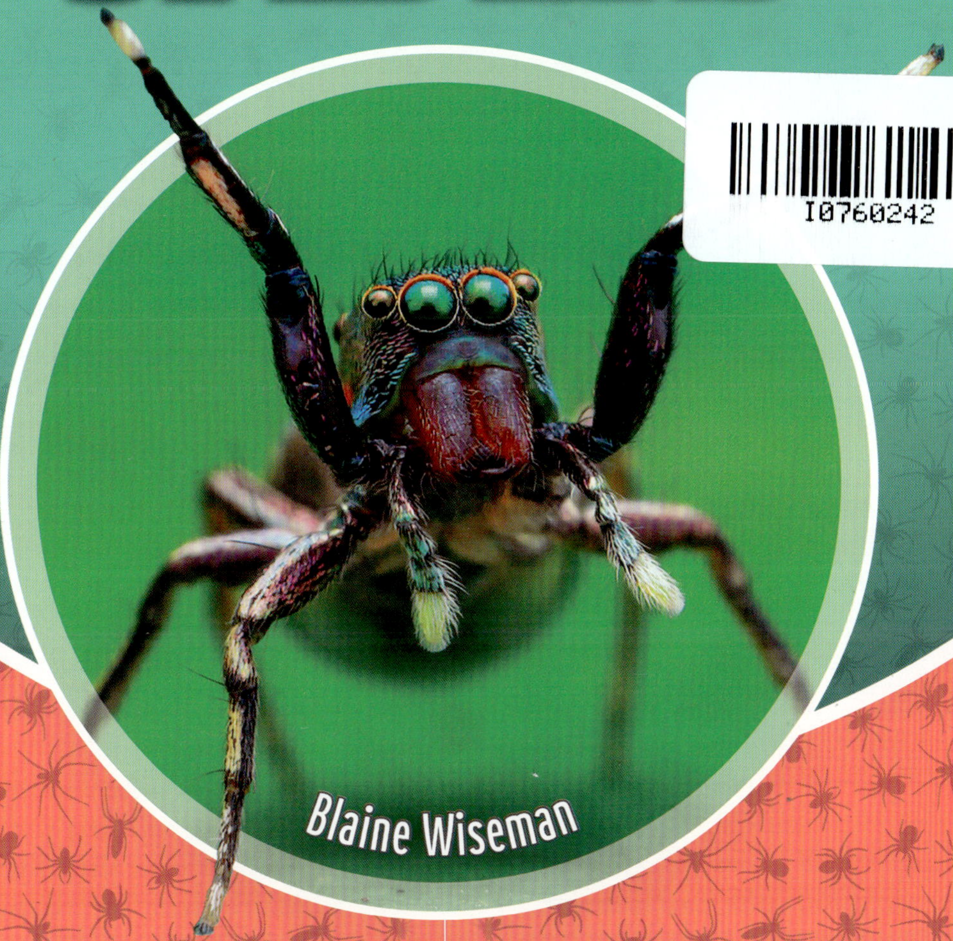

Blaine Wiseman

SPIDERS

www.av2books.com

Step 1
Go to **www.av2books.com**

Step 2
Enter this unique code
BTVPAK2Y9

Step 3
Explore your interactive eBook!

AV2 is optimized for use on any device

Your interactive eBook comes with...

Contents
Browse a live contents page to easily navigate through resources

Audio
Listen to sections of the book read aloud

Videos
Watch informative video clips

Weblinks
Gain additional information for research

Try This!
Complete activities and hands-on experiments

Key Words
Study vocabulary, and complete a matching word activity

Quizzes
Test your knowledge

Slideshows
View images and captions

... and much, much more!

SPIDERS

JUMPING SPIDERS

Contents

Introduction

The Nimble Jumping Spider

Jumping spiders spend their time being still and watching the world around them. They have excellent eyesight. This helps them find **prey**. It also helps them see when danger is near.

When it is time to go, jumping spiders move quickly. They get their name because they can jump long distances.

Jumping spiders have the best eyesight of any kind of spider.

Parts of a Spider

What Jumping Spiders Look Like

Jumping spiders are small spiders. They are usually no longer than 1 inch (2.5 centimeters). Like many spiders, they have eight legs and eight eyes.

Two pairs of eyes are on the top of the spider's head. Two more pairs are on the front. The two middle eyes are larger than the rest. The back part of a jumping spider's body is called the abdomen. It is where the spider's silk is made.

Jumping Spider Life Cycle

Most jumping spiders only live for one year. Males often have colorful markings and patterns on their bodies. This helps them find a **mate**. Sometimes, males use motion to look for mates. They raise their front legs and dance.

A female jumping spider lays her eggs in an egg sac. She guards them until they hatch. After they hatch, **spiderlings** leave the nest to find their own homes. As spiderlings grow, they **shed** their skin.

Sizing It Up

Zebra Jumping Spider
Leg Span: 0.3 inches (0.8 cm)

Western Black Widow Spider
Leg Span: 1.5 inches (3.8 cm)

Carolina Wolf Spider
Leg Span: 3 inches (7.6 cm)

Giant Golden Orb Weaver
Leg Span: 5.9 inches (15 cm)

Giant Huntsman Spider
Leg Span: 12 inches (30.5 cm)

Goliath Birdeater
Leg Span: 12 inches (30.5 cm)

What Big Eyes You Have

Jumping spiders hunt in the daylight. They need light to see clearly. The two large eyes at the front of a jumping spider's head give it excellent forward vision. They help the spider jump at moving targets.

The smaller eyes at the top of the spider's head let it see to the side and back. This helps a jumping spider move safely in any direction.

What does a jumping spider see?

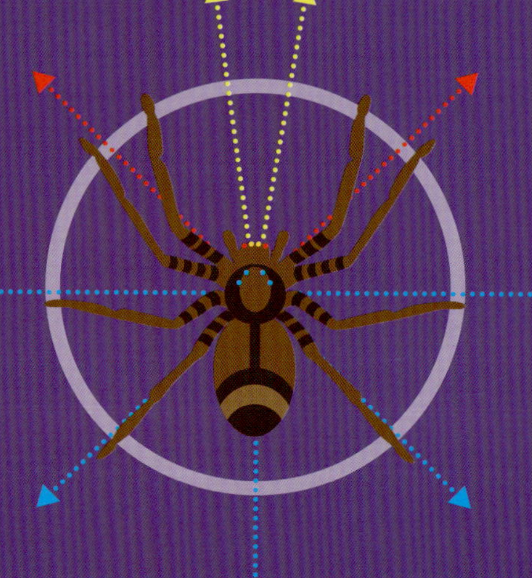

The different eyes of a jumping spider allow it to see all around itself.

What a Drag

Instead of building webs, jumping spiders jump to catch their prey. However, they still make silk.

Jumping spiders use their silk as a **dragline**. They attach it to where they are standing before they jump. If jumping spiders miss, they can safely climb back up the dragline. This keeps them safe from dangerous prey such as wasps or other spiders.

Jump Around

Jumping spiders do not have the **muscles** that humans and other animals use to jump. Instead, they use their blood.

A jumping spider can quickly fill its legs with blood. This forces the spider's legs outward and launches it into the air.

Some jumping spiders can jump distances 50 times their body length.
Jumping spiders may hunt animals up to three times their size.

Map

Where They Live

Jumping spiders are found all over the world. Most live in **tropical** areas. However, many can be found in cold places, too. Jumping spiders have **adapted** to many different **environments**.

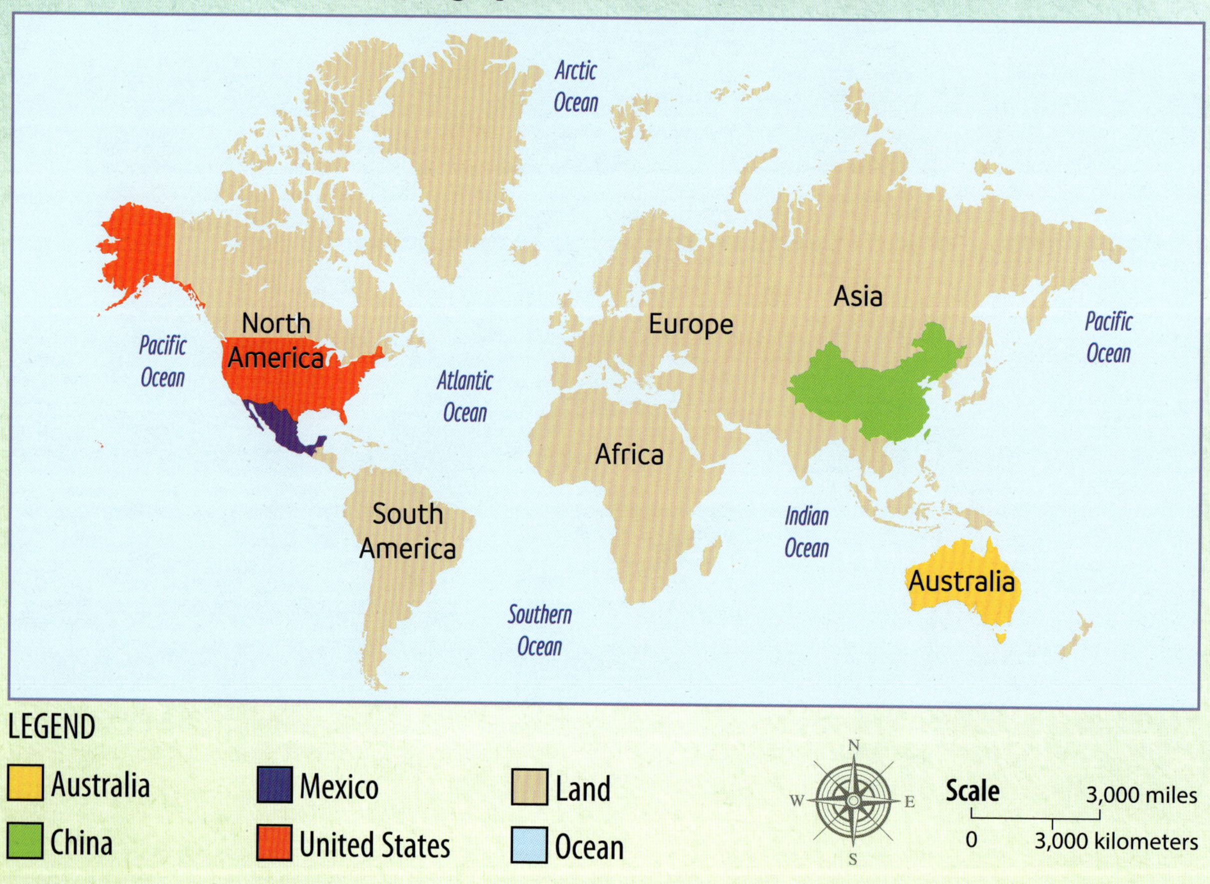

Bagheera Kiplingi

Bagheera kiplingi is the only spider in the world that mostly eats plants. This jumping spider is found in Mexico. Part of its name comes from Rudyard Kipling, the author of *The Jungle Book*. The other part comes from Bagheera, a character from the book.

Zebra Jumping Spider

Zebra jumping spiders are found around the world, including all over the United States. They are hairy with black and white stripes, like zebras.

Himalayan Jumping Spider

The Himalayan jumping spider lives at higher **elevations** than any other spider. It has even been found on Mount Everest in Nepal and China.

Fringed Jumping Spider

The fringed jumping spider is known as a very smart spider. It hunts other spiders on their own webs. Fringed jumping spiders live in many countries, including Australia.

Jumping Spider Safety

Most spiders will run and hide from people. However, jumping spiders may jump onto a person's hand. This is more dangerous for the spider than for the human.

Jumping spiders are **venomous**, but they do not usually bite. Their fangs are small. Only people who are **allergic** to jumping spider venom can be hurt by them. Jumping spiders are helpful animals. They eat many **pests**.

Activity

Create a Spider

There are many different kinds of spiders in the world. They all have certain features in common. However, each spider also has its own features. They help the spider live in its home.

Make your own spider by answering the following questions:

1. What is your spider called?
2. Where does it live?
3. What features does it share with other spiders?
4. What features help it live in its home? How do these features do this?
5. What does your spider look like?
6. Use pencils, markers, or crayons to draw your spider living in its home. Make sure to include all of its features.

Quiz

Test Your Knowledge

1
What is the back part of a spider's body called?

2
What percent of the world's spiders are jumping spiders?

3
What is a baby spider called?

4
When do jumping spiders usually hunt?

5
Do jumping spiders build webs?

6
Which jumping spider is known for being very smart?

7
Which jumping spider is found on Mount Everest?

8
Are jumping spiders dangerous to most people?

ANSWERS 1. The abdomen 2. 13 3. A spiderling 4. During the day 5. No 6. The fringed jumping spider 7. The Himalayan jumping spider 8. No

Key Words

adapted: changed over time to live in a certain area more easily

allergic: people whose bodies react badly to certain things

dragline: a line or rope attached behind something moving

elevations: how high things rise above the ground

environments: surroundings

mate: one member of a pair of animals that can reproduce, or have children

muscles: parts of a body that can tense or relax to move it

pests: animals that are harmful to or unwanted by humans

prey: animals that are hunted

shed: when an animal loses a layer of skin in order to grow

spiderlings: baby spiders

tropical: parts of the world that are mostly warm all year

venomous: an animal that uses toxic chemicals

Index

Get the best of both worlds.

AV2 bridges the gap between print and digital.

The expandable resources toolbar enables quick access to content including **videos**, **audio**, **activities**, **weblinks**, **slideshows**, **quizzes**, and **key words**.

Animated videos make static images come alive.

Resource icons on each page help readers to further **explore key concepts**.

Published by AV2
14 Penn Plaza, 9th Floor New York, NY 10122
Website: www.av2books.com

Library of Congress Control Number: 2019957569

ISBN 978-1-7911-2300-0 (hardcover)
ISBN 978-1-7911-2301-7 (softcover)
ISBN 978-1-7911-2302-4 (multi-user eBook)
ISBN 978-1-7911-2303-1 (single-user eBook)

Printed in Guangzhou, China
1 2 3 4 5 6 7 8 9 0 24 23 22 21 20

052020
101119

Designer: Terry Paulhus Project Coordinator: John Willis

The publisher acknowledges Alamy, Dreamstime, Getty Images, iStock, Minden Pictures, Shutterstock, and Wikimedia as its primary image suppliers for this title.